You are vvords

County Council

Libraries, books and more . . .

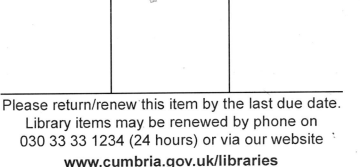

2 8 AUG 2015
0 3 DEC 2015
1 6 MAR 2017

Published by the
Journal of Dementia

You Are Words – Dementia Poems
First published in 1997 by
Hawker Publications Ltd
Culvert House
Culvert Road
London SW11 5DH
Tel 020 7720 2108, fax 020 7498 3023

© John Killick 2011

Second edition 2008
Reprinted 2009, 2011

British Library Cataloguing in Publication Data

A Catalogue in Publication Data

ISBN 978 1 874 79090 7

Designed by Jay Dowle and Sue Lishman
Revised by Andrew Chapman

Printed and bound by DG3, London

The Journal of Dementia Care is published six times a year by Hawker
Publications. For further information please contact Hawker Publications
(address above).

Other books by John Killick published by Hawker Publications:

Openings (dementia poems and photographs) John Killick & Carl Cordonnier
(ISBN 1 874790 49 3)
Dementia Poems (audio CD) Readings exploring the experience of memory loss,
from *You are Words* and *Openings* John Killick (ISBN 1 874790 76 6)
Dementia Diary (poems and prose) John Killick
(ISBN 978 1 874 79087 7)

Contents

FOREWORD

I want to thank you for listening.
You see, you are words.
Words can make or break you.
Sometimes people don't listen,
they give you words back,
and they're all broken, patched up. (p10)

John Killick's work has made two very special contributions to the cause of good practice in dementia care. Giving time and concentrated attention to an individual, listening carefully to what they say, tells each person with dementia they are valued, that they are of interest and worth. The further step of writing down what is said powerfully underlines that statement of worth. For the person with dementia this is a rare, maybe unique experience. John Killick's confidence in people's ability to communicate (even those who are severely damaged) has been rewarded with communications of clarity and intensity from people who care staff thought could hardly talk at all.

Then, his paring down of the words into what seem to be the most illuminating, essential trains of thought, compels us to focus on these words in a way that we (staff, carers, friends and relatives) usually find very hard. We find it hard for several reasons. The culture of 'busyness' in care work, where sitting down and listening is not seen as real work, may be changing but is still widespread. Listening well is an emotionally demanding activity. It is also hard in the normal course of life to focus on the essentials amid a stream of words that seem incoherent. But as poetry the words make sense, in riches of metaphor and meaning.

These poems are a powerful argument against the myth that people with dementia cannot communicate, that they lose their personalities and therefore become non-persons. The fully human status of those who speak in these poems shines through in their individual voices, their resilience, insight, wit and creativity. Absorbing this message is as vital a part of professional education as formal textbooks and training; therefore I believe this book should become essential reading in dementia care.

Sue Benson
Editor, *Journal of Dementia Care*

INTRODUCTION

'WHO'S IN CHARGE OF THE SPARE WORDS?' — a question to me from someone with dementia. The words of someone who obviously felt the need to express himself, but was painfully conscious that the capacity to articulate his perceptions in language which either satisfied himself, or succeeded in making contact with another human being, was slipping away. That, in short, is what dementia does to people — it progressively robs them of a lifetime's stored memories, and the means of communicating their needs in the present. It is a terrifying process to watch, let alone experience. This book constitutes an attempt in poetic form to explore this phenomenon from the inside.

The poems have their origin in an unusual collaboration: that between poet and a number of individuals with dementia. Between 1992 and the present I have been writer in residence for Westminster Health Care, a nationwide provider of nursing homes for elderly people. Most of the pieces date from the period commencing February 1994 when I embarked on a two-year project working largely with the mentally ill, part-funded by the Arts Council of England. I worked in over thirty nursing homes in England, Scotland, Wales and Ireland. Some of the poems reflect their geographical origin in turns of phrase and the use of dialect words.

I do not believe it is important for the reader to be in possession of clinical details of the various illnesses suffered by the authors. What is important is to recognise that all those represented in this collection have dementia in some form or another. In reading the poems we are therefore gaining insights into the states of mind and feelings of a hitherto largely unrepresented and neglected section of society.

Our culture is one which still puts great emphasis on the word, both written and spoken. In particular, our ability to articulate our thoughts and feelings is used as an indicator in ascribing status to individuals. Older people in our society already experience a devaluing because of loss of work role and of purchasing power. Those with dementia, because of their communication problems, occupy an even less favoured position. This has an adverse effect on their own self-esteem. Struggling to cope with the disintegration of their language skills, they tend to find what statements they do manage are misinterpreted, or, worse, ignored.

It is hardly surprising that we have been vouchsafed few examples of writing by those with dementia, because of the extreme difficulty of obtaining them. Most of the individuals represented here could not have written down their poems even if they had wanted to do so. Among the other capacities that have deserted them is that of writing. Of the handful who were still able to put pen to paper, writing poems was almost certainly an activity beyond their experience. So these poems have been written for them out of their own words. But even that task was fraught with difficulties.

Dementia breaks down the speech patterns of individuals until the faculty may be lost altogether. With a handful of the people I worked with language abilities were still intact. With the majority coherence was intermittent. With a few it had almost gone, and it was a matter of waiting for the occasional moments of lucidity to occur. I have tried to represent all three groups in the work chosen, but I have resisted the temptation to arrange the poems in any kind of progressive (or regressive) order. So a transparent piece of writing may be found alongside a poem in which conventional structures and vocabulary have begun to disappear.

A significant characteristic of the speech of many people with dementia is the direct expression of emotion. The disease has a disinhibiting effect and so the barrier to speaking directly of one's feelings has been swept away. At the same time intellectual capacities are diminished, and rational language proves elusive. Suddenly talk blooms with metaphor, allusion, the currents of feeling are reflected in rhythm and cadence. I have no doubt that the natural language of those with dementia is poetry.

There is a sense in which the exact authorship of these poems is a matter for dispute. In one way it is mine, for the constant element in this collection is my presence transcribing, selecting and shaping. The poems inevitably reflect my personality and approach because they would not have come into existence without that participatory element. But equally, not a line would exist without the experience of the people I worked with. All the statements, questions and exclamations which fill these pages were compiled from transcripts of conversations with residents. I don't believe there are many spare words here.

In my role as craftsman I have attempted to pare language away to lay bare the preoccupations of individuals. You could say that in some instances I was attempting to make clear the essential nature of the confusion.

I will quite rightly be asked what criteria I have employed in making this selection. Some of these will, I hope, become clear in the commentaries with which I introduce each group of poems. But in general terms I have certainly not attempted to provide a kind of freak-show for voyeurs of altered mental states. Nor have I been concerned to feed researchers with materials. I hope the general reader for whom this book is intended, especially the increasing number of people whose lives have been touched by dementia in some way, will by reading through these pages gain a vivid picture of the effects on personalities and outlooks of this degenerative disorder. But apart from such enlightenment I would wish to make the claim that the best of these poems, in their economy of expression, their emotional honesty, and their metaphorical exactness, are real poems, and therefore, in however small a way, constitute a contribution to literature.

John Killick

Acknowledgements

I should like to thank the Linbury Trust for a grant which enabled me to work on the text of this book at Stirling University. Also my colleagues at the Dementia Services Development Centre there and Dr Richard Cheston at Bath University for valuable criticisms of the first draft of the manuscript. Thanks too to the Arts Council of England for two-year grant aid and to Westminster Health Care for support throughout the whole time I have been working as a writer with people with dementia. My deepest gratitude goes to those whose thoughts and feelings are represented in these pages.

Further reading

Killick J (1994) *Please give me back my personality!* Dementia Services Development Centre, Stirling.

THE POEMS
Listening and writing

The book begins with three reflections on the processes of listening and writing down what is given. The statement 'YOU ARE WORDS' which provides the collection with its title can be regarded as a compliment to the writer, and I certainly took it as such at the time, but it clearly has wider implications. The way we speak to each other is crucial to our functioning as human beings: selection of vocabulary, volume, tone and so on, are the means whereby we convey attitude and caring as part of a communication. It becomes even more important in speaking to people with dementia because of the problems they may be having in coming to terms with the illness and in making themselves understood.

The feelings expressed by the speaker of 'You Are Words' might usefully be placed alongside those of the speaker of 'Problems' (especially the last verse). The speaker of 'Writing it Down' shows that he understands the importance of trying to compile a life history. He is also someone who seems to have attained some composure in the face of the deterioration in his mental condition. We shall meet others later in the book.

YOU ARE WORDS

Life is a bit of a strain,
in view of what is to come.

Sometimes I feel embarrassed
talking to anybody, even you.
You don't really like to burden
other people with your problems.

I have been a strict person.
What people and children do now
is completely different. Any beauty
or grace has been desecrated.
The circle of life is shot away.

I want to thank you for listening.
You see, you are words.
Words can make or break you.
Sometimes people don't listen,
they give you words back,
and they're all broken, patched up.

But will you permit me to say
that you have the stillness of silence,
that listens, and lasts.

PROBLEMS

I have a problem:
I have a house on either side of the road,
but I only have a room in one of them.
How do I cross the busy road?
And what happens if I break down in the middle?

I have another problem:
I've spilt something on my skirt.
There's nothing there?
Are you sure there's nothing there?
Well it must have been in another room.
Well it must have been in the other house.
Well it must have been another skirt.

And I have a problem about kindness:
A lot of those who come round here
are not interested in being kind to others.
Kind is the only thing one can do here.
It is all there is that can help.
I don't *try* to be it.
You shouldn't have to *try* to be kind.

WRITING IT DOWN

It's a good idea,
this writing it down;
it's got a bit of merit.
It's tantamount to saying
you're speaking from your memory all the while.

In the War I went around
and I saw nothing that wasn't
a waste of time and life.
The door opened to dust
and I thought it might be me tomorrow.

Such unselfish lives,
just putting themselves last
in all walks. No bitterness
or anguish, all loving-kindness.
Now the evening is coming to its close for me.

You don't see your family
much now: like a carrier-bag
on your back, one way or another.
But you can't barge it or dish it —
all of it was everwell.

Life stories

The next three poems all constitute attempts at life stories; none of them is successful. The first person's mind is too quick for him; it jumps about too much, though he does in the last verse acknowledge the therapeutic nature of the process. The second person's mind moves too slowly, and the effort taxes him greatly; he offers some revelations, but is unable to provide any detail, and cannot perceive a pattern in his past experience. The third person is suspicious, and is reluctant to proffer what little he does recall.

By contrast the speaker of 'Bell Lane' has a very clear long-term memory, and provides a vivid snapshot of her urban childhood. The last piece in this section 'From My Hiding Place' is full of pictures of a rural childhood. There are some confusing references here, but on the whole it is a fascinatingly intricate meditation. It ends with a moving reference to the speaker's mind as a refuge from current problems; she is comparatively lucky, because many of those with whom she shares this book find no comfort even in their memories.

LETTING IT ALL OUT

I've got no money.
I emptied my pockets because
if I don't they'll get pinched.

Mum's dead. Dad's dead.
Everything's sold up.
I've got a marvellous wife, though.

And then there's the toast.
Artificial teeth top and bottom.
Even cut up I can't chew it.

I had a nice bike, nice pair of brakes.
I was caught by the police
riding without a licence.

Pain in my chest right across
means I have to take it easy,
go at my own pace.

Say I was who I am,
and you're doing what you're doing,
d'ye think my wife would come?

Write me your name and address,

and don't let me lose it,

so you keep it for me.

Opened the door, let it all out.

That's about all for now.

Put 'etc. etc. etc.' for the rest.

THIS IS A LIFE STORY, ISN'T IT?

This is a life story, isn't it?

This is where I have to start digging deep?

I was born into a railway family.

It's all part of life, I say.

I've always been interested in trains.

I think now I'll have a little sleep.

I got a woman in the family way.

Other people have a lot more brains.

My mother was a very strong believer.

You know, life's not all fun and games.

I loved a married woman once.
But that's part of another story.

I had a friend who was a fitter.
Other people have a lot more brains.

I had a son who committed suicide.
It's all part of life, I say.

My mother couldn't walk after a stroke.
You know, life's not all fun and games.

My grandson plays cornet in a brassband.
But that's part of another story.

You ask, why did I come in here?
This is where I have to start digging deep.

I don't think of the days that have gone.
I don't think of the days to come.

This is a life story, isn't it?
I think now I'll have a little sleep.

I CAN'T TELL YOU

I can't tell you
how many times
I've been knocked over.

I can't even give you
the name of
my condition.

I was an engineer.
In a manner of speaking
I still am.

I can't even give you
the name of
my qualification.

I think maybe
you know as much about me
as I do myself.

I think maybe
I've told you far too much
about myself already.

BELL LANE

You won't find me as one
as goes deliberately missing.
You won't find me as one
that swanks with half-a-dozen in my hand
to keep them sweet.

I went to a Board School.
My teacher was nasty and sharp.
But the Headmistress,
she was a real angel.
'Guardian Angels'
is what I call the place.

Tell Tale Tit
Your tongue shall be split
And all the dogs in town
Shall have a little bit.

Where will we run to?
Up Bell Lane.
I'll tell the teacher
And you'll get the cane.

I have a book in my room
full of innuendoes.

Of course in them days
they were staunch
and would never tell where you'd gone.
We'd run up a long street
that had been grassed over,
with wooden railings on either side.
But there were steel railings
running down the middle.
It was a dangerous place to play.
My mother would shout:
'Get up them stairs
and stay there!
And no jam butties tonight!'

Bell Lane's still there.
We'd push our prams up it.
I could go with you straight,
and I don't think we'd have a gate to climb.

FROM MY HIDING PLACE

You give it as you talk.
There's no-one saying it
or doing it in a certain time.
You take it and make it your own.

There have been other loves
but none like that of my mother.
She had birds that came onto her hand,
pecked, and flew away.

What a wonderful time! —
we were brought up that way.
She was very particular
how and where. I shall not forget.
She would make little noises
and then pull it in —
the string of humankindness.

The wind started to come
and I didn't know whether
to come in here or to go out there.
My mother stood at one door.
Nasty blows came over the water.
We had to prepare very quickly.
It all came rushing down from the top.
I liked the rush and the bush!

My father was a man that spent
his life with all that was spread.
He was a beautiful man.
I looked up to him.
He would walk a mile
to rescue one little chick
he thought was on bad legs.

If anyone came to the gates
he would get hold of their head
and shake it from side to side
and tell them not to come again.

The farm was rather a nice grey.
Everything that walked and moved
and would follow me I loved.

Dogs are my best, and
I like the small ones. They do
what I say without
any ums or ahs.

I used to play cricket.
I was good and could go anywhere,
if I had the whizzer.
I never did see
where the red balls came from.

To a degree I've been the boss.
No children of my own, but
for my own: up the road
and down the dale I'd go
three times a day.

If I must be honest,
it took such a long time
to get to know them — some 16-year-olds
— it was all flying away from them,
so we had to start over.

But there was always a certain time
when a certain little boy
was having that certain little thing
that was there for him.

We gave things to them
where they had been lacking.
We showed them how to laugh.
And they never forgot my name.

Twice and twice over
what I think is important.
My hiding place now is one
that I can stretch out to
and run away to for a while.

Feelings of panic

The next three individuals are all confused to the extent that they experience feelings of panic. It is difficult to imagine what it must be like to be conscious that one's grasp on reality is slipping, and that there is nothing that you or anyone else can do about it. It may be that this is only a stage in the development of the disease, this half-way house between normality and a new less aware state, but this does not make it any the less frightening for the sufferer.

'Find Me' is probably the most immediate expression of this dilemma that I have encountered. The Scottish lady in 'Sad Refrains' keeps repeating herself, and this provides the structure for her lament ('to greet' is to cry). 'The Key' could be about a real object, and in a sense it is, but surely it is also a metaphor for the mechanism which unlocked the subject's mind to himself and helped him make sense of his predicament? In which case that key is now lost, and he has to look for new ways to attain peace of mind.

The fourth speaker expresses a state of mind that is common in people who do not have the disease; it is not clear whether the lady feels low because of her dementia or it is something that she must suffer in addition to it. Again she is a Scottish speaker ('to ken' is to know). The poem ends with a vivid metaphor for her condition.

FIND ME!

I can't place
this place at all...
isn't that terrible?

What street is this,
what town, where is
the nearest post office?

Can you take me
home so far?
I'll reward you.

I can't find
that label with my
name and address.

Find me! Find me!
I wish to God
God would do something!

SAD REFRAINS

I've greet 'n greet 'n greet...

I was aye one for singin' in the Chapel.
We were a' guid singers in ma family.
'There is a green hill far awa'.
I've aye been in a Christian place a' ma life.

I hope it a' comes quicker'n I think.

I dinna ken whit I've done. I dinna ken
whit I'm daein' sittin' here. I'm shair
ma man's in the hoose. And ma daughters.
And their bairns. I aye like wee ones to carry to.

I've greet 'n greet 'n greet 'n greet...

I wouldna be beholden to naebody.
I wouldna interfere wi' naebody's business.
I wouldna hurt naebody, no' me.
So why'm I nae hame? I've been here nearly a' day.

I hope it a' comes quicker'n I think.

We've a' been set up as Christian Pedants.
And ma mither wi' ainly one leg!
I wouldna hurt a hair. I wouldna hurt a bairn.
I've aye been in a Christian place a' ma life.

I've greet 'n greet 'n greet 'n greet...

It's gettin' dark. I've been here nearly a' day.
I havena a purse nor naethin'. I dinna ken
whit I've done. I've done naethin'.
I'll hae to be gettin' back to ma man.

I hope it a' comes quicker'n I think.

THE KEY

Have you any openings?
Have you got a guide?
Could you come along
and turn a key in a lock for me?

You'll not find my room.
I've only got... nothing.

This my room? Not mine.
Not my room.
Not my clothes.
Not my bed.

I'm going home.

DEPRESSION

I'm on the edge wi' it.
It's just the feelin' that's
come inside o' me, when
we were waitin' to get in.
It's not a funny thing,
it's just a shoutin' thing —-
why do they come like that?

It's like I've done too much,
but I havena' done oniethin'.
Mebbe I've always been runnin' too much.
Mebbe I've always been kennin' too much —-
nae need to, I ken.
What I do feel is this:
too thin 'n too this 'n that.

It's your head first,
then your heart,
then your legs...
you seem to feel everythin'.
I feel it even in my hands, you ken?
It's like you're on a roundabout,
but it's inside o' you.

Nursing homes

The next section deals with the stresses and strains of being in an institution. The demands of caring for people with dementia often become so severe that relatives find themselves unable to cope, so many sufferers are admitted to nursing homes. Of course all the people I have worked with are in such establishments. Adjustment to being on a unit with twenty or thirty other people with the disease can often be painful.

A person already experiencing confusion may find the surroundings of the nursing home bewildering. This is what the first lady expresses in 'This'. A rather different reaction comes from the speaker of 'Home'; she well understands her situation and makes some sharp comments (this poem also contains a remarkable example of figurative language in verse five). In 'No Help' the speaker feels oppressed by the staff and having to obey the rules, whereas the reaction of the man in 'Ally' is to rebel; he sees the writer as a friend whom he can trust and with whom he can indulge in plotting.

The Welshman in 'It's a Place, In It?' is perhaps rather limited in his responses, but he perceives that routine does not allow for the regular refreshment he craves. In a more sophisticated way, the speaker of 'Finding Fault' articulates the same need; he is caustic in his jibes at staff, and scathing about the building — perhaps these are reactions to the idea of incarceration? In the next piece the lady flays her fellow-residents with her tongue; but maybe in the last two verses she reveals rather more about herself than she realises. Finally, 'Grass' is a touching lyric from someone who longs to be away and in the countryside.

THIS

This is the strangest place.
I'm sure it isn't me
that's gone round the bend.

I don't understand a word
or an action here
that shows the face of the people.

This is all bedsitterdom.
It's like a little town.
But whose town is it?

In my own mind
I only came here yesterday.
I have no clue whatsoever.

This is happening, isn't it?

HOME

I've lived here since the War finished.
It's a nice place and nice people, but it isn't home.

That man is completely up a gum tree,
but he'll be able to get down again.

That's one of the children in the playground crying.
Her parents are here looking after her.

That door's squeaking. It hasn't very much sense.
It makes you wonder who's looking after it.

There were people here yesterday who had the pull with us,
but then they had to let their ropes go.

There's a party coming in tomorrow
which will make this place overcrowded.

There's so much space down below
that it seems ridiculous not to use it.

I think it's a pity to have all these people together in here.
They don't wear as well as they would outside.

NO HELP

I'm not to ask for any help.
They've told me, I'm not to ask.
They told me up the corridor.
So I'll do as others do:
I'll just go to sleep.

I can't have any help.
No wonder, there is none.
She came through
when they were telling me
so she knows.

Can I get undressed?
Be careful, they might hear you,
you can't be too careful.
I'm not to get washed or that —
Orders of the Management.

They don't give you a chance:
if you do this you'll get that;
if you do something else you'll get the other.
I'm not asking any questions,
I get jumped on every time.

ALLY

I'm not doing nothing here.
I was punched beaten and robbed.
I'm almost blind now.
And I'm not receiving you.

I've been a fighting man.
And in the pubs too.
I've got a lot of enemies.
And I need an ally.

If anybody asks you
say that you're my brother.

A friend of mine's in here now.
He's not much cop to no one.
I've been here nearly a year
and I don't have a penny off of them.

Him's the Big Samaritan,
as the fella said.
Him's the Lone Ranger,
that's about his height.

If anybody asks you,
say that you were working.
My late father knew that fella.
Worked in Nooney's the Undertaker's.

He done them for years.
Then he went quick enough himself.

I don't like leaving my wife too long.
I've been married fifteen years.
You say that that's not long.
I say that that's too long.

If anybody asks you,
say that you were looking me up for injuries.

I'll tell you what I'm doing.
You'll get such a shock.
You'll see my photograph on the wall.
I'm doing picture-work for everyone.

If anybody asks you,
say that you were just leaving.

This place is a school,
but they learn you nothing here.
There are not men like yourself,
men that you can talk to.

If anybody asks you,
here's what you should do:
shut mouth and catch no flies.
Shut mouth and cut this very quick.

IT'S A PLACE, IN IT?

Well, I'm good. I live not far from here.
Can you get me a cup of coffee after?

It's a place, in it? Oh dear, oh dear!

The fair used to come to Mr Leonard in his field.
I never worked for them. I worked on his farm, see?

I've a pullover. I've had it a couple of years.
And when am I going to get a cup of tea?

The fair used to come in with trucks and cars.
And they'd go at night to the rides, two at a time.

I love a few pints. And a smoke too, ha ha!
And a cup of tea when it comes round.

I'm in a pullover, see? And I don't feel the cold.
And the food's good. And plenty of friends around.

It's a place, in it? Oh dear, oh dear!

Single I am, yes, and happy. And I don't know
what year I was born. Seventy? Well, it's a guess.

I've got a pullover, see? And I can't handle
a cup very easy. But I might get one soon?

You don't smoke at all? Well, I do,
two or three. And I do take a cup of coffee.

Ok, now I'm being good. I live not far from here.
So I might get a biscuit? And a cup of tea after?

It's a place, in it? Oh dear, oh dear!

FINDING FAULT

Have you ever tried not interrupting people?
It would thrill you to the bone!
Actually I'll talk to anyone
so long as they observe the proprieties.

You don't write shorthand?
Of course writing shorthand or not is your concern.
Your ability to do whatever you are doing
is nothing to do with my ability to do what I am doing.

In this place all the cups of tea
end half-way up. If I get tea
in a saucer anyone can have it.

What I want to know is:
is there any limit to when I get the top half?

The object of golf is to hit the ball
as fast as you can, direction immaterial.
I've never owned a set of clubs
and I've never owned a trolley.
The truth is I'm here on a golfing holiday
and they haven't even got a course!

This isn't a building, no way
is this a building. I'd describe it
unkindly. Somebody came along
and stuck three rooms together
and called it 'A Home'!
Then 33 other people came along
and each tacked a piece on.
In short, it was thrown together
and the bits didn't meet,
and'll never be got right.

The best way to improve this place is...
bigger cups! And I don't know whether
that's my view of tea or golf!

A TOUR OF THE MENFOLK

That man's supposed to be my father,
but there's no more wrong with him than your boot.

My mother would say that that man
has a mouth like a chicken's arse.

And that man's the biggest rogue in creation:
the sooner he's under the dirt the better.

That man, I tell you, he's absolute craft,
and he tells lies like Tom Pepper.

That one comes out with a string of swearings.
If I catch him he'll get it across the kisser.

That man's my brother-in-law. He's always trying
to hitch it with me, but I'm not having any.

And that man, his character goes before him.
Like mine does. But I'm a Christian.

I get on with all of these men alright.
And if they want to do anything

I tell them how: that the best way
to get on in life is to agree with me.

GRASS

A young fella carried me
in here, it were a long way
and a long time ago.
I were lying on grass...

I don't want to stay, no
there's nothing for me
they're all very kind
but I don't want to be

inside anywhere at all
it's much too hot and bright
it just don't feel right
I've not been used

I need the fresh air
I keep calling out:
nurse, nurse, carry me
outside to where

I were lying on grass...

Using language

The next three poems are examples of individuals giving free rein to the affective uses of language. The first two appear to be about disempowerment: in the first loss of employment leads to loss of role. The speaker compares his situation unfavourably with that of the writer, who is perceived as still having a job. It may also be that the barrow stands for something larger than this: maybe 'I never carry as full as you do' refers to concepts of coherence and autonomy.

Certainly the speaker of 'Monkey Puzzle' feels that everything about her existence has become 'managed' without consultation. This poem constitutes probably the most fierce and outspoken attack upon certain adverse effects of life in a home of any of the speakers. The monkeys would be a metaphor for those persons appointed to be in charge of her. She rages against the arbitrary nature of their decisions and wholly rejects their authoritarian stance.

The speaker of the third piece seems only to be able to conceive of his existence in terms of a catalogue of all the objects that he has known. He is obsessed with the material nature of the world. Or is it that, lacking the capacity any longer to follow a logical train of thought, he has fallen back upon free association, for sometimes there appears to be a linking principle, but as often it is some intuitive resemblance, or even the sound of a word that suggests the next link in the chain of naming.

THE BARROW

Have you seen my barrow?
I joined the group,
and now it belongs to all of us.
But I don't know where it's gone.

It seems as if
I'm like a buzzing toy —
it buzzes round and round
but it doesn't mean much.

Altogether you won't find
much toing and froing
and doing or being
with me. I never carry
as full as you do.

The way this country's going
men can just go round
and do as they choose.
They can take my bed
and my barrow.

I think I just drift about.
I think that's what I do
usually. I'm just a kind
of quiet nobody.

MONKEY PUZZLE

I'm suffering from the Monkey Puzzle.
The Monkey Puzzle is this place.
The Puzzle is: how to cope with the Monkeys.

I can't remember anything of today
except the peppering of my tongue. Yes,
my mouth was peppered again this morning.
I believe it is part of the Monkey Puzzle.
These little Monkeys have two legs,
you know, and wear suits.

These whiskers that are growing
around the lower part of my face,
I did think they formed a part
of the category of the Monkey Puzzle,
put there to irritate newcomers.

I've come to the conclusion
that what we should do
is educate these Monkeys.
We should make it perfectly clear
that there are certain things
that are not done, even though
I know that they are laughing
their heads off behind my back.

People are pushing things down my neck.
I don't believe it's even for a joke —
it's pure badness. Next time anybody says
'Put that in your mouth!' I'll take a flying leap
and punch them. It's an unignorable fact
that they are mucking me about.

If this is another bit of the Monkey Puzzle,
then Monkey will know what it's got!
I'll run amok a-shutter, I really will,
I'll just go wild and frighten them!

THE NAMING GAME

I used to play the arpeggios and the overtures.
My brother Jack would sing it straight off.
'Will o' the Wisp', 'Whispering'.
And then you've got 'The Birth of the Blues'.

You've got Mutton Chops, Pork Chops, Pork Dripping,
Lard, Margarine, Butter, Butter Beans.
Now Marjorie grew some beautiful flowers
In her greenhouse. And tomatoes too.

You've got your Sunlight Soap, Saline Drip, Crumpsall Biscuits,
Crimplene, Cashews, Rose-coloured Flowers —
I used to take a bouquet of a dozen roses
To my mother when she had the babby.

You've got Sun Shades, Umbrellas, Lemonade
(great big bottles), Butterscotch, Scotch Whisky —
When my Uncle Albert was top public
He won a Scholarship, pure thoroughbred.

There's Brass Bands, Cornets, Wafers, Blocks,
Choc Ices, Whipped Cream Walnuts, Boxes of Dairy Milk —
My mother would buy a quarter a week,
And my father had one ounce of plug tobacco.

You've got your Beddings, Nottingham Lace Curtains,
Carpets, Woollen Blankets, Wooden Tops, Turnip Tops,
Spinning Tops, Trampolines, Heavy Mattresses, Beds that
When you put your feet down you get cold ones at the end.

Bandages, Band Aid Clubs, Puttees, Putting Greens,
Flags of all the Nations, Hat Pins, Pin Tables,
Plus Fours, Pincers (with their Movements), Pliers,
Planks of Wood, Woodchoppers (with their Balls).....

I never felt so well — it's the laughter,
It keeps me young, it beats all the drugs.
I've always told the truth. And in this
That has truly been my intention.

Family relationships

Family relationships assume great importance for people with dementia. 'Grieving' provides a reminder that people with the disease have needs which must be addressed which they have in common with others of a similar age, in this instance to come to terms with events at seventy years' remove!

'Mother to Son' is about a relationship in the here-and-now. The mother pours out her frustration to her helpless offspring (in reality a fifty-year-old man who retired emotionally wounded from the scene, leaving his mother to seek reassurance from myself, repeating over and over the question 'I am a nice person, aren't I?') The most significant part of her outburst is surely the lines 'All I'm interested in/ is my life's going' and it is revealing that in the end she recognises her anger towards her son as having been in some sense 'worked up'.

There is a fear expressed by many people that, as family members die, they are going to be left to soldier on alone. The speaker of the last poem seems determined to claim me as part of her family, however remote.

GRIEVING

Nearly seventy years since that day
and I got over the first shock
then on with my life. Now I
feel the need to become reconciled
with my father's death in some way.

Afterwards my mother asked
my sister 'Do you remember him?'
To which she replied 'No,
was he the poorly man in the bed?'
But I think I have not done with grieving.

I must see about it straightaway.
I shall go to the place and buy
a posy of flowers to place on his grave.
Can you understand how I cannot
rest until I have made this peace?

MOTHER TO SON

Come back to me!
Every sentence I speak to you
you take no notice!
Where are your cigarettes?
You've given them all to him!
Get your trousers out!
Get your trousers out
and put them all in one bag!

All I'm interested in
is my life's going.
If you've been told once
you've been told a thousand times!

Get me in, will you!
Let me get going!
You can go and see Sister
or anyone you like.
Fasten your effing belt!
Are you going
to let them all go,
or are you going
to go and see about something?

She's addling in that!

You won't get it!

It's all gone to Auntie Margaret!

Get your overalls on,

and get your things!

You needn't bother

to sit with me!

I shall just scream

the bloody place down!

The truth is mine not yours!

Dargie is a liar,

and he's a bigger liar than Tom Pepper!

Get down and burn them!

See to it now!

I don't give a bugger

what anyone hears!

I'm standing here

trembling from head to foot,

and it's hard work!

KEEPING IT IN THE FAMILY

You didn't have a house in them days, you had rooms.
I came to live around this part, and it's a nice part, isn't it?
Now I've a house with two rooms to spare.

Are you my uncle then?

The girls were nice. Not like now when they get a bit hoity toity.
My girls quarrelled, it got a bit touchy at times.
I think it's better if you get strangers bringing them up.

You are gran's father then?

My grandmother never seemed never to make nothing hard.
My dad was a very strict man. Still is.
My man never comes in and grouses, nothing like that.

Are you one of the sons then?

All those old'uns'll be gone, spent their days.
Old people today don't try to do what they shouldn't.
If there's anything here I try to keep it on the level.

Are you a bit of a relative then?

Self-portraits

The next five pieces are all portraits of their speakers. The characteristics are revealed as much in how the individuals express themselves as in the actual statements they make. They constitute, in my view, a powerful contribution to the personhood debate: the idea that dementia results in the stripping down of personal characteristics versus the view that it does not.

'Peachey' positively bubbles, she radiates optimism; when handed her poem she immediately sought out an audience to declaim it to. The speaker of 'Man-mad' made her preferences very clear in both word and deed, but I escaped with my prize: the poem!

The lady in 'Summer's Day' was the opposite of predatory: she was all serenity and poise, and these qualities even inform the structure of her piece. 'Him' is a Welsh lady providing a portrait of a man, but also, of course, of herself. All the speakers in this section are female, as are the majority of the people represented in this book. But this reflects the situation in the population generally: because of their longevity the number of women with dementia heavily outnumbers that of men. 'Thirteen Snapshots' speaks for itself: another lively, humorous lady, like Peachey, but more quirky and grasshopperish.

PEACHEY

When we got off the plane
the man in the little hut
was selling the photographs he took.
He said 'This is the lady.'
He didn't need any building-up of acquaintance.
It was straight from the horse's mouth.

I wasn't brill at school,
but the boys called after me.
The boys christened me 'Peachey'.
They'd say 'Tell Peachey'.
And I didn't like it.
I didn't know it was a gift.
But the teacher had a soft spot,
he never said anything, of course,
but it was in his eyes.

I roar with laughing at people,
and they laugh at me.
But I don't know any jokes.
It's all home-made humour.
If it fits I say the phrase.
Sparsmodic. I can laugh and like it.

I used to sing for the people,

sing what fits the emotion at the time.

When I first did it

I thought I was going to be reprimanded

for singing out of line.

But Life is Singing.

I'll talk, but it's not my scene,

chatting somebody up.

I'm not a grabber of situations.

I come out in little phrases, that's me.

And I don't know anybody who's not cheerful.

I bet you've never been so near Nature before!

MAN-MAD

You're awful. It's you.

I'm a terror. That's true.

But I do like being with you.

You're soft and cuddly,

you are, but I don't like

behaving in here.

I've no shoes on,

but it don't matter.

I've no tights on,

but it don't matter.
I'm not off anywhere.
Let me kiss you. Come 'ere.

I love you. 'Man-mad' —
my husband has said
that many times. He's had
hard times to cope. Comes sometimes.
You'll see him in the woods
when we go there.

I don't know about you.
But I do trust you.
And I take to you.
I take to you in 'ere.
And I'd take you in the woods
when we go there.

When I saw you I come.
I just wanted to hold
and hold you one minute.
And then another two.
And then told
my daddy what you done.

SUMMER'S DAY

How nice to see you again!
That tie you are wearing is beautiful.
I wonder, is it Primrose Day or something?
I believe my mother used to celebrate Primrose Day.

We all appreciate it very much
your visiting us. You may not think it
when you perhaps arrive at the wrong moment,
but we do like to see you.

I would wish to offer you a cup of tea.
When people come to the house
it is the first thing you think of.
We were brought up to it.

It is a perfect Summer's Day.
But are those rain clouds or shade clouds?
It would be a lovely day for boating,
when you've a lovely river like we have.

We've got the river, and the lovely
country, and the hills on either side.
It would be a very nice day for boating.
And we could call in for a cup of tea.

You look so cool in that shirt and tie.
It is a Liberal colour, but paler,
a Liberal colour, a lovely colour —
how kind of you to wear it for us today!

HIM

Ach away! He's awful!
Don't ask him in!
The second day he started:
spit everywhere! They put a glass
in the door to see where he comes.

They lock all their backdoors
in case he comes in.
There's a shed outside
in which he keeps everything.
He's comical. And dirty:

his face and hands —
dirt keeps them warm!
Forces himself in,
he's rude and cheeky.
And like a horse eating.

He's the town's trouble.

He should be in a cage.

Beats his wife, you know,

when he takes the drink inside him.

And when he's sober.

Put the book in your pocket,

every last word of it.

Go now, go straight.

And call next weekend.

I'll have more cleck for you then.

THIRTEEN SNAPSHOTS OF MAISIE

Hullo, you're more welcome
than the Duke of Edinburgh!
My mother likes you — she says
you're alright, so that's something.

*

Have you a cigarette
to dry up this hay fever?
Ten or five will do.

*

Am I married? No,
I was waiting for you.
I'd love to do the tango
but you might break in two!

*

Middlesbrough's a big place
with quite a few factories.
They started putting things in cupboards,
and it developed from there.

*

I've had a busy time
while you've been gone
painting all the doors white.

*

Oh this damned hay fever —
if you haven't a cigarette
to dry it up it don't
half give you some stick!

*

My mother has a beautiful house.
I am very houseproud too.
But I've got this big hole
in my trousers at the knee,
and it really bothers me —
torn on the arm of a chair.

*

Any time you want a ride
on a horse my son's got two.
And if you ever want
some clean notes in your hand
he works in a bank.

*

Have you got a car here?
Then you can take me home with you.
What'll your wife say?
'Oh, I see you're a bigamist!'

*

The shades on these lamps
two or three weeks ago
were all hanging over
but I put them straight.

*

Where's your pipe today?
What, you don't smoke?
Then you must be a Presbyterian.
I've seen your picture in the paper.
My, you look just as young
as you are. You can see
your toothie-pegs, man,
that they've been cleaned!

*

Have you a cigarette?
Thank you. You'll get nun for this.
You don't know what to do with a nun?
There's nothing to do with one,
because it's nun yesterday,
nun today, and nun tomorrow!

*

If you'll still be here
when I get back
that'll please me:
I'll put a tick by your name.

Confusion

The next two pieces exhibit a higher level of confusion than any others in the book. Both ladies are unable to sustain their thoughts or their language structures, and both are given to that behavioural activity that is often referred to as 'wandering'. Some people see this as purposeless, but just as their speech exhibits clear signs of effort in an attempt to clarify meaning, so, in my observation, does the restless movement stem from a search, perhaps to obtain physical reassurance from surroundings which continually deny it to the individual.

Both poems win through to sentences of mysterious power or clarification. In the first the lines are 'I didn't know if you would understand,/ with you living on the other side.' Does this refer to the home, or sanity, or some perceived language barrier? Or, since this is poetry, all three at once? I only know that at the time, as I have experienced with many of the other people whose words fill this book, I did not feel myself to be on the other side of anything from her. The last line of the second poem encapsulates one of the effects of dementia in a most touching manner.

ON THE OTHER SIDE

I'm just going round to see what's round the corner...

I've lived here twenty-five weeks in the city,
up and down the language, twice up and down...

I'd better just have another look...

I'll tell you if you can understand the language.
And I'm talking, talking all the time...

I'm just off to see if it's changed at all...

I didn't know if you would understand,
with you living on the other side...

I'll just see if it's all right over there...

Young girls wearing white on the other side
of their dress getting married...

I'll just see if I can get far enough along...

WANDERING

I'd have liked to be in this
of yours. I feel I wasn't quite
last time, though I tried.
I'm not much good at this.
I think you'll have to do
all the work yourself.

Most times you've got to laugh,
but sometimes you can't laugh.
Sometimes I get a bit overcrowded.

I don't talk to others a lot.
I speak to my own family,
but not all the time.
I don't often speak to my family
now because I really mean to
but it very seldom happens.

I just tell them no,
and I don't for a minute
admit the fact that...
I don't want them to think...
I don't even let them know...
this and that comes into my mind.

It's a bit funny in places:
I thought the time was going to go
off, but it's still carrying on.

They tell me my age,
when they take my photos and that,
and half-an-hour later,
d'ye know, I can't remember.

I've been out wandering a bit.
I'd better go and see
if there's anything from home.

That's a nice little piece
of writing you've done. It's better
that, love, than nothing.
I hope it does something for you.

My memory, it slims away.

...and finally

The final section contains two of the most complex and remarkable poems. The speaker of 'Nae Oniethin' is a Scots lady who may well be suffering from another mental illness besides dementia, and has spent much of her life in institutions. There are some strange assertions here, yet there are also passages full of insight: the verse about the Mona Lisa, for instance. But it is the piling up of negatives which gives this piece its rhetorical force.

'I Scream' is a very sophisticated poem, and I did not impose this structure upon it, it arose naturally. It is a monologue in which the speaker makes use of the highly literary device of quotations (from nursery rhyme and popular song) which are counterpointed against each other to reinforce the message of marital breakdown. That the person has been an actress makes the dramatic patterning even more convincing. The modifications of meaning in the last three lines are especially subtle.

'Freedom' comes from the same person as 'Grieving' and 'Monkey Puzzle' (the only speaker to be represented more than once in the book) and ends the collection on a note of resignation.

NAE ONIETHIN'

I couldna spin a web.
Only a spider could do that.

I've never had a happy life.
I've never had a good time.
I didna take my porridge,
but my mother smacked my backside
till I was sair and cryin'.

My godfather was the nicest man
that ever was born. Every fountain,
every well was his.
And every farmsteading.
He had hay fever and asthma.
He hid everything in a shed.
If he got a chair he never sat on it.
He was aye staundin' with his haunds at his back.
He was never with oniebody.

In Elocution and Poetry I had nae lessons.
I never took a medal. If I did
I didna ken. I never took
the top seat. The Matron
wasna' oniebody, she thieved everything.

There was a man in her room.
She put a hand doon his troosers.
He got it. I wasna' there.

I was married. I got a ring.
It was my ain, but I never had it on.
He was a secret agent and a spy.
I wasna' lang wi' him.
I wasna' lang wi' oniebody.
I never spoke to him ever.
He never signed.
Nae man ever fancied me. It was
an Immaculate Conception.

In Gay Paree I went to see
The Mona Lisa. She never laughed
or smiled or did oniethin' like that.
Naebody lookin' like that
ever loved.

That parrot on my TV,
it's a speaker on the top.
It says 'I'm sayin' naethin'.
I've never said anythin' ever.'

I'm nae here. I'm nae
better. I'm nae oniethin'. I am that
for which the nurses have nae cure.

I havena' given you oniethin'.
I've given you damn all.
I'm nowhere at hand.
I'm no nor nothin'.
I dinna look in a mirror
and admire myself.
I dinna smile nor drink.
Nor speak to oniebody.
I'm nae oniethin'. I *can't* be.

I SCREAM

'It's a Long Way to Tipperary' —
but I can't remember the words.

I was a very lively little girl.
I always loved jumping about.

I like children like ice-cream.
'Ice-cream, you scream, we all scream'.

'And My Heart's Right There' —
see, I've remembered another line!

My husband was a doctor.
The children rushed about calling him daddy.

I was lucky to get that husband.
I've kept the pictures, and everything.

'Goodbye, Piccadilly' —
that's another line.

I used to be on the stage when I was young.
Not singing. It was a long time ago.

I get pain now all the time.
'Ice-cream, you scream, we all scream'.

'Goodbye, Leicester Square' —
and another line!

It's a lovely ring my husband gave me,
but it's not a token of his love.

It's all finished between us.
We don't talk to each other now.

'It's a Long Way to Go' —
that's another line!

I don't know what this place is.
I don't know who these people are.

We're a nice two-lot, you and me.
I like us being with us.

'It's a Long Way to Tipperary' —
that's the line we started with!

It's nice to have a laugh.
It's nice when somebody talks to you.

'Ice-cream, you scream, we all scream'.
A nice doctor. A nice barrel of fun.

'It's a Long Way to Tipperary,
It's a Long Way to Go' —

It's a long time ago —
It's a long time no go.

FREEDOM

Are we all kidnapped?
I'm not at all sure
what kidnapping is, but
I know I'm very frightened.

I could go out there
and sit on that swing
and I would enjoy it.
I want my freedom.

But we none of us have our freedom.
I don't understand so much,
that I'll just do without it,
chuck the whole lot in the air.

Postscript

A literary critic to whom I showed these poems expressed disappointment. 'They're not mad enough,' he said. I was shocked by his reaction, but later decided that it was probably an accurate reflection of the stereotype of dementia which many people have. To me the fact that his impression was of the lack of 'madness' was encouraging. For too long negative attitudes have held sway and the 'madness' of those with dementia has been a self-fulfilling prophecy. What I find most positive about these poems is that they make it more difficult to come out with black-and-white judgements in this area. Every piece here has aspects of what those of us without the disease recognise as life as we live it. But almost every piece also has elements which we might label 'out of the ordinary'. It is because of this ambiguity, this mixture of the familiar and the strange, that the poems, it seems to me, pose challenges.

First and foremost, they pose a challenge to the idea that dementia destroys the personality, and leaves a blank where there was an individual. Surely every speaker here is sharply discriminated from every other by perceptions, tone of voice, use of language?

Then, for all their humour, their poignancy, their insight, these utterances have the capacity to make us feel humble and rather uncomfortable in their presence. The underlying question they ask is 'What is normality?' and they demonstrate the narrow line between the concept we cling on to and the other possibilities that crowd around asking to be recognised.

But is it possible to read them and not be moved to the extent of offering help to these speakers? That is the third challenge that they pose. If we can empathise in this way, if the poems make us see that 'they' are so like 'us', then surely the 'WORDS' are both a release for those with the disease and their feelings, and for our own capacities as human beings? The next stage must be to let their spirit inform our actions and help to create a new culture of caring.

Index of first lines